DISASTERS

Mount
ST. HELENS

Jen Green

GARETH**STEVENS**
PUBLISHING
A WRC Media Company

Please visit our web site at: **www.garethstevens.com**
**For a free color catalog describing Gareth Stevens Publishing's list
of high-quality books and multimedia programs, call 1-800-542-2595 (USA)
or 1-800-387-3178 (Canada). Gareth Stevens Publishing's fax: (414) 332-3567.**

Library of Congress Cataloging-in-Publication Data

Green, Jen.
    Mount St. Helens / Jen Green.
      p. cm. — (Disasters)
    Includes bibliographical references and index.
    ISBN 0-8368-4498-X (lib. bdg.)
      1. Saint Helens, Mount (Wash.)—Eruption, 1980—Juvenile literature.
    2. Volcanoes—Washington (State)—Juvenile literature. I. Title: Mount
Saint Helens. II. Title. III. Disasters (Milwaukee, Wis.)
    QE523.S23G74   2005
    551.21'09797'84—dc22   2004056711

This edition first published in 2005 by
Gareth Stevens Publishing
A WRC Media Company
330 West Olive Street, Suite 100
Milwaukee, Wisconsin 53212 USA

Original copyright © 2004 The Brown Reference Group plc. This U.S. edition
copyright © 2005 by Gareth Stevens, Inc.

Project Editor: Tim Cooke
Consultant: Frank Ethridge, Professor of Geology, Colorado State University
Designer: Lynne Ross
Picture Researcher: Becky Cox

Gareth Stevens series editor: Jenette Donovan Guntly
Gareth Stevens art direction: Tammy West

Picture credits: Front Cover: United States Department of the Interior, U.S.Geological
Survey, David A. Johnston Casacades Volcano Observatory, Washington, Vancouver.
Corbis: Bettmann 7, Douglas Kirkland 22; OAR/Undersea Research Program: P. Rona/
NOAA 14; Topham: Corporation of London/HIP 20; United States Department of the
Interior, U.S.Geological Survey, David A. Johnston Casacades Volcano Observatory,
Washington, Vancouver: title page, 4, 5, 8, 9, 11, 12, 13, 18, 21, 23, 24, 25, 26, 28,
29t, 29b; USACE: Bob Heims 27.

Maps and Artwork: Brown Reference Group plc

Printed in the United States of America

1 2 3 4 5 6 7 8 9 09 08 07 06 05

ABOUT THE AUTHOR

Jen Green holds a doctorate in English and American studies. She has been
a children's author for over twenty years and has written more than one
hundred books for younger readers on many subjects, including history,
geography, and natural history. She lives in the south of England.

CONTENTS

1 THE DAY THE SKY TURNED BLACK

In early summer 1980, scientists in the United States knew there was a danger that Mount St. Helens, a volcano in Washington State, might be getting ready to erupt. What no one guessed was just how big the explosion would be. Its effects were felt over a large area of the Pacific Northwest.

On May 18, 1980, just before 8:30 A.M. on a Sunday morning, a horrifying sight sent scientist David Johnston racing for his radio. "Vancouver, Vancouver, this is it!" he shouted into the microphone. Johnston was working for the United States **Geological** Survey (USGS) as a geologist, a scientist who studies rocks, soil, and minerals and what they tell us about Earth's history. Johnston was on a ridge just 5 miles (8 kilometers) north of Mount St. Helens, a volcano in the Cascade Range in Washington. The USGS scientists believed the volcano was ready to **erupt**. Now Johnston saw the north side of the mountain collapse in a giant landslide. The long-awaited eruption had started.

▶ **A cloud of ash rises from Mount St. Helens just after the eruption at 8:22 A.M. on May 18, 1980.**

▼ **Before the explosion, the peak of Mount St. Helens, in Washington State, was a popular place for tourists to visit.**

4

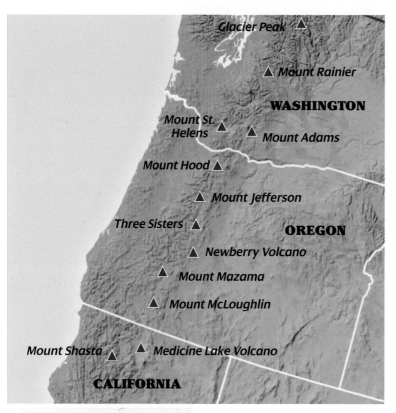

◄ **This map shows the location of Mount St. Helens in the Cascade Range in Washington State. It is one of the youngest of the chain of volcanoes in the Cascades.**

The landslide marked the start of one of the strongest eruptions ever recorded in North America. A small earthquake triggered a huge explosion that blew away the north side of the mountain. Clouds of hot ash, steam, and gas eventually turned an area of 230 square miles (596 square kilometers) into a gray, ash-choked wasteland. The eruption continued for four days, showering ash over the Northwest and smothering nearby towns and farmland. Smaller eruptions continued until 1986. Before the 1980 eruption, Mount St. Helens had been quiet for over a century. From 1831 to 1857, small eruptions had shaken the mountain without doing much harm. Since then, the mountain had been silent, and its Native American name, Tahonelatchah, or "Fire Mountain," was almost forgotten. The park around the snow-capped peak had become a magnet for nature-lovers. Deer, elk, cougars,

THE MAN WHO STAYED WITH THE MOUNTAIN

In spring 1980, all of the people who lived on Mount St. Helens left—except for one man, Harry R. Truman. With his wife, Edna, Harry had built a tourist lodge and cabins at Spirit Lake, below the mountain's north side. When Edna died in 1978, Harry stayed on, and now refused to listen to warnings to leave. On May 18, a tide of ash, dust, and rock engulfed Spirit Lake, raising the water level by about 200 feet (60 m). Harry got his wish never to leave the mountain. He and his lodge now lie buried deep below the lake.

▼ Surrounded by souvenirs of his life, Harry R. Truman explains to reporters why he refused to obey the order to leave his home.

THE ERUPTION FROM THE AIR

Geologists Keith and Dorothy Stoffel had a terrifying view of the Mount St. Helens eruption. They were watching the gently smoking volcano from a small airplane when Mount St. Helens erupted. As the ground began to "ripple and churn," they realized they were in grave danger and urged their pilot to flee. The little plane sped away just as a giant column of dark ash shot upward from the mountain's peak. Flying at full speed, they managed to outrun the dark cloud and landed safely, shaken but alive.

▼ Geologists look dwarfed by the trees knocked down by the Mount St. Helens eruption. The blast knocked down enough timber to build 150,000 houses.

black bears, and mountain goats roamed the tree-covered slopes and grassy meadows. Trout and salmon swam in cold streams and lakes, attracting fishing fans. Despite the decades of quiet, geologists knew that the volcano was one of the most **active** in the Cascade Range. By 1980, the experts predicted that a big eruption was due.

ANIMAL WARNINGS

Animals seem to behave in strange ways before disasters such as eruptions or earthquakes. The eruption of Mount St. Helens was no different. Half a minute before the eruption, beavers on a pond 35 miles (56 km) away slapped their tails on the water in warning. As the blast was heard, they dove below the surface. Such incidents suggest animals can sense danger. They may be reacting to movements in the ground or other changes that humans cannot sense.

By March 1980, Mount St. Helens had begun to puff dark plumes of smoke. On its north side, an outcrop named Goat Rocks began to bulge out. For geologists, these were warning signs that magma (red-hot, **molten** rock) was rising underground to fill the hollow below the volcano, where it was trapped by a cap of hard rock. Gas in the magma made it likely to blow up. David Johnston said the mountain was like a keg of gunpowder, saying, "The fuse is lit, but we don't know how long [it] is." At 8:22 A.M. on that bright morning, the powder keg exploded.

READY TO BLOW

After a warning from USGS scientists, park officials had set up a 20-mile (32 km) no-go zone around the mountain. Only geologists could go inside. Everyone else had to watch the eruption from outside the danger area.

► These mailboxes for homes located near the Cowlitz River were almost totally covered by the mud that swept down the river valley after the eruption.

► **This map shows the area that was covered by lava and debris after the eruption.**

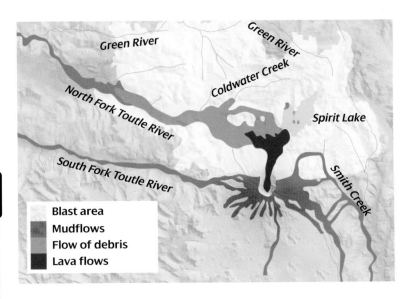

Green River

Green River

Coldwater Creek

North Fork Toutle River

Spirit Lake

South Fork Toutle River

Smith Creek

Blast area
Mudflows
Flow of debris
Lava flows

EYEWITNESS

"The cloud [moving toward me] was laden with violent thunder and lightning and the sour smell of sulfur. Moments later, the cloud had taken over the entire sky, and the heavy ash began to rain down, heavy like sand . . . gritty. The thunder and lightning was terrifying, there was so much of it and so close at times. That sunny morning turned to darkness, and just for a moment I recalled Mount Vesuvius with the same cataclysmic action. It was frightening to think this could possibly be our fate as well."

– Patricia Nesland

Throughout April and early May, Mount St. Helens disappointed people waiting to see the eruption. Then on May 18 it finally blew—but with a force no one had predicted. The first earthquake knocked off the rock cap that had trapped gas and magma inside the mountain. As the pressure was released, the mountain exploded with a deafening bang that was heard about 200 miles (320 km) away in Canada and California. The force it gave out was five hundred times greater than that of the most powerful bomb dropped during World War II.

THE MOUNTAIN ERUPTS

In seconds, Goat Rocks and the north face of the mountain slipped away in the greatest landslide ever recorded. The explosion blasted ash and gas to the north, west, and east, creating a fan-shaped zone of destruction that

EYEWITNESS

"I had just started to drive onto the overpass (over Valley Freeway) and there it was. It was almost like a motion picture or, more accurately, a painting. There was such a surreal feel to it all, it was like watching the end of the world coming slowly and you could do nothing but watch."

— Lee Harris

was 8 to 15 miles (13 to 24 km) wide. Many thousands of trees were snapped like matchsticks. On Coldwater Ridge, David Johnston had no chance. The blast threw him off the ridge with his truck. His body was never found.

Streams of super-hot ash and rock ran down the mountain. Spirit Lake and about 130,000 acres (52,600 hectares) of land were buried by a blanket of burning ash. After the first blast to the side, the force of the eruption turned upward. It blew about 1,300 feet (395 m) off the mountain's peak. A huge column of ash, gas, and steam rose into the air. It leveled off to form a vast cloud lit from within by lightning.

The tide of ash melted snow and ice on the mountain's peak. The water and debris mixed

► **A helicopter stirs up ash as it lands near Mount St. Helens a month after the disaster. Ash fell in eleven states.**

11

▲ **The young USGS geologist David Johnston relaxes at his base camp on the mountain the evening before the eruption.**

to form deadly **mudflows**. Rivers became fast gushes of mud. Floodwaters tossed trucks and bulldozers aside like toys. Three hundred homes were buried by mud or swept away.

LUCKY ESCAPES

A total of fifty-seven people died in the Mount St. Helens disaster. However, many more had lucky escapes. Geologist Dan Miller was due to join his workmate David Johnston on Coldwater Ridge, but a camera repair delayed him from leaving long enough for news of the disaster to reach him. Meanwhile, a team of loggers working just 5 miles (8 km) south of the crater was also unharmed. The loggers counted themselves extra lucky in their choice of work site on that fateful morning. Just a day earlier, they had been working on the north side, and would have been caught within the fan-shaped zone of total destruction.

Soldiers from the **National Guard** and other emergency workers rescued scientists, fishermen, and campers from the mountain. Helicopters and emergency vehicles saved a total of 198 people, but 57 people died.

RAIN OF ASH

Millions of tons (tonnes) of ash that had been flung up to 12 miles (19 km) in the air began to fall back to earth. For hours, it rained over a huge region including parts of Washington, Idaho, and Montana. Within days, the ash cloud had reached the Pacific and Atlantic coasts. Yakima, Washington, 85 miles (136 km) east of the volcano, was the worst-hit town. Its citizens watched as a giant cloud blotted out the sun, and darkness fell at 9:30 A.M. Schools, restaurants, and stores closed as a thick layer of ash settled on streets and buildings.

▼ **This car was swamped by ash over 10 miles (16 km) away from Mount St. Helens itself.**

13

2 WHAT ARE VOLCANOES?

Volcanoes are weak points in Earth's outer crust. Molten rock beneath the crust, called magma, forces its way to the surface. At weak points, it bursts through the surface or triggers eruptions of gas and ash.

When super-hot magma comes to Earth's surface and cools, it is known as lava. Some volcanoes are long cracks in the crust, called fissures, where lava spreads into wide, low ridges. In other places, lava builds into tall, cone-shaped peaks like Mount St. Helens.

About fifty years ago, scientists discovered that Earth's crust and upper mantle are made up of about twenty stiff pieces that fit together like a huge jigsaw puzzle. These pieces are called **tectonic** plates. The plates float on a hot, partly liquid layer below them, called the mantle. The plates sometimes smash into each other, pull apart, or scrape past one another.

▼ **Black smokers are midocean springs caused by volcanic activity on the bed of the sea.**

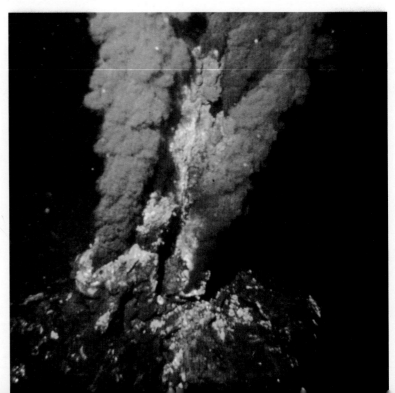

14

EARTH'S STRUCTURE

▼ This diagram shows Earth's interior. The activity that creates volcanoes happens in the lower mantle.

crust

upper mantle

lower mantle

outer core

inner core

Geologists believe that Earth's interior is made up of layers. The hard outer layer, called the crust, is the thinnest at between 4 and 43 miles (6 and 69 km) thick. In proportion to the earth's total size, it is about as thick as the peel on an apple. The thick layer below, called the mantle, is solid at the top in the upper mantle and molten (partly liquid) in the lower mantle. Some scientists believe that slow-moving currents in the mantle force magma upward to form volcanoes. Earth's center consists of an outer and inner core, probably made of iron, where temperatures may be as high as about 9,000° Fahrenheit (5,000° Celsius).

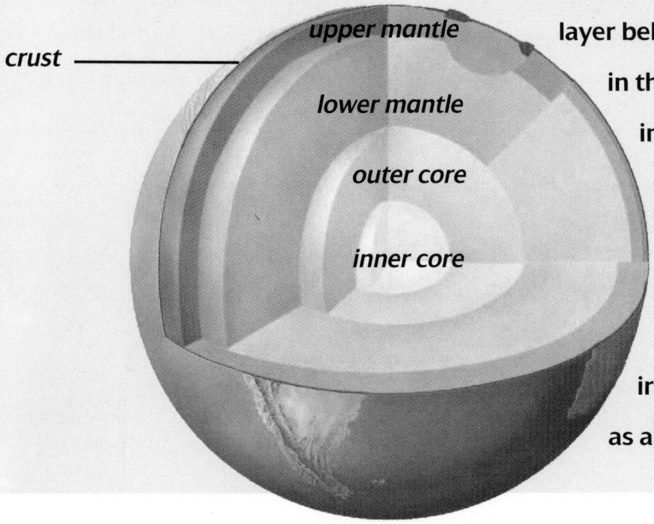

Volcanoes and earthquakes happen where plates meet, where Earth's crust is often the thinnest. Volcanoes also erupt in the middle of plates at weak points called "hot spots."

Such huge eruptions as Mount St. Helens are rare, but each year, around twenty to thirty volcanoes are active on land and more erupt beneath the oceans. Many volcanoes are located in ridges on the seabed, which mark places where plates are pulling apart. Lava wells up through the cracks to form new crust, creating the ridges. The activity at these ocean ridges creates springs called black smokers,

15

THE RING OF FIRE

▼ This map shows how the volcanoes called the Ring of Fire surround the Pacific region.

Earth's crust is made up of seven huge plates and about a dozen smaller ones, which fit together like a jigsaw puzzle. Many volcanoes push up along the borders between plates, especially along the rim of the huge Pacific plate beneath the Pacific Ocean. This boundary is called the Ring of Fire because of the large number of volcanoes located along it, including Mount St. Helens.

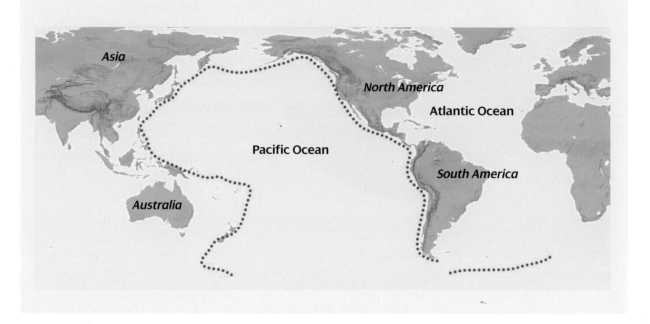

which spout super-hot clouds of water and minerals. Scientists discovered the existence of smokers in 1977.

Mount St. Helens is one of a chain of volcanic mountains that runs down the West Coast of North America, from British Columbia, Canada, to California. Over millions of years, the mountains were pushed up in a chain following the Pacific coast because, offshore,

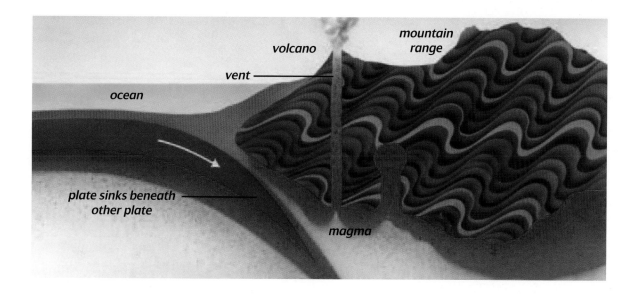

ocean

volcano

vent

mountain range

plate sinks beneath other plate

magma

tectonic plates smashed together. About 70 miles (110 km) out to sea, an ocean-bearing plate collided with the plate bearing North America and was pushed beneath it. Deep in the hot upper mantle, the plate that was pushed down melted. The molten rock then rose again to the east to form the Cascade Range, including Mount St. Helens.

STRUCTURE OF A VOLCANO

Before a volcano erupts, magma rises by filling cracks and faults and by melting rocks in the mountain. Gas and water also collect underground, and the pressure builds. Finally, the hot materials push upward through a weak point, which becomes the central vent, or opening, of the volcano. Side vents also allow magma to reach the surface, where it erupts as lava. When the volcano erupts, clouds of boiling-hot gas,

▲ This diagram shows how volcanoes form above an area where one of Earth's plates is pushed down beneath another. As the rock melts, it rises to the surface through weak points in Earth's crust. A place where one plate sinks beneath another is called a **subduction zone.**

17

steam, and ash made of tiny rock pieces may be flung high in the air or roll in clouds down the mountainside.

TYPES OF VOLCANOES

Active volcanoes are erupting or have erupted recently. Dormant, or sleeping, volcanoes may not have erupted for centuries, but will one day become active again. Mount St. Helens was one example of a dormant volcano. Volcanoes that are unlikely ever to erupt again are called "extinct." Supposedly "extinct" volcanoes surprise experts sometimes by coming back to life, as in 1961 when the "dead" volcano on the South Atlantic island of Tristan da Cunha suddenly began to spout ash and lava.

▼ **Surrounded by steam rising from the crater floor, scientists take gas samples in a volcano. Gas from small vents is a good way to judge what is going on inside the volcano.**

VOLCANO SHAPES

▼ These diagrams show four of the different shapes volcanoes take mainly because of the type of lava, number of vents, and the tectonic activity in the area.

Magma forms volcanoes of different shapes. Cinder cones have a single vent and often violently erupt lava that becomes pieces of cinder, which settle close to the vent and build up. In shield volcanoes, runny lava gently spills out around the vent before becoming solid, creating a low, flat cone. The lava in lava domes is so thick, it hardly flows and builds up over or near its vent. Composite volcanoes, such as Mount St. Helens, build up layers of lava and ash until the vents are plugged, then they may blow.

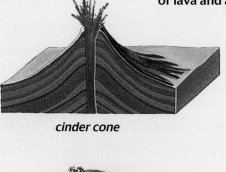

cinder cone

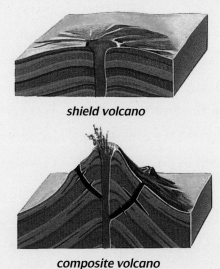

shield volcano

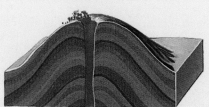

lava dome

composite volcano

WATCHING VOLCANOES

Scientists who study volcanoes are called volcanologists. They have the sometimes dangerous job of trying to predict when volcanoes will erupt. Scientists use a variety of instruments to work out what is going on inside volcanoes. The instruments include seismometers, which are machines that measure earthquakes that often happen just before eruptions. **Tiltmeters**, laser beams, and gravity meters can detect changes in the shape of the mountain. Volcanologists also study gas and water samples near volcanoes for signs of underground activity. The lessons of Mount St.

PAST ERUPTIONS

One of the most famous eruptions in history was the eruption of Mount Vesuvius in Italy in A.D. 79. The disaster was seen by a Roman writer called Pliny the Younger. A tide of ash and mud buried the town of Pompeii and the village of Herculaneum located on the plain below and killed thousands of people. In 1883, the volcanic island of Krakatau in Indonesia blew up with a roar heard about 3,000 miles (4,800 km) away. The eruption caused huge tidal waves to sweep across the ocean, drowning villages on neighboring islands. About thirty-six thousand people died. In 1902, a disastrous eruption struck the Caribbean island of Martinique. When the volcano, called Mount Pelée, erupted, fiery clouds engulfed the port of St Pierre. All of the thirty-eight thousand townspeople died but one—the survivor was a prisoner protected by the strong walls of a jail.

▼ **This painting was made in the nineteenth century to represent the explosion of Mount Vesuvius in A.D. 79.**

▶ **Mount Shasta in California rises above mounds of debris blown all the way from Mount St. Helens in Washington State.**

Helens helped improve the prediction of when volcanoes will erupt. Scientists watching the peak had placed many instruments around the mountain to pick up signs of an eruption. Puffs of smoke and gas rising from the crater, rocks bulging on the north side of the mountain, and earthquakes all suggested that magma was rising inside the mountain.

Since 1980, the study of volcanoes has improved thanks to new instruments. Today, geologists can put information about rock bulges, earthquakes, the release of gases, and other data into powerful computers, and the computers give instant results predicting when eruptions might strike. This allows officials more time to take action.

3 AFTERMATH OF THE DISASTER

After the eruption, plants and animals soon returned to Mount St. Helens. Cleaning the ash from town streets did not take long. New roads and guards against flooding were built on the mountain, along with new centers for visitors.

After the eruption on May 18, 1980, cleanup operations began. About 600,000 tons (544,000 tonnes) of ash were removed from the streets of Yakima, Washington. Orchard owners used helicopters, sprayers, and sticks to knock ash from fruit trees. Damage to crops cost $175 million. Loggers harvested the fallen timber that littered the mountain's sides.

Ecologists studied the amount of damage to the region's wildlife. Many creatures had died in the eruption, including thousands of elk and

▼ Like snow, gray ash coats the street of a town in Washington State in the days following the eruption of Mount St. Helens.

22

▲ A U.S. Army Corps crane clears mud and ash from the Toutle River in February 1981. The eruption dumped so much debris in the region's rivers that some rivers had to be closed to ships.

deer, as well as smaller mammals, birds, and reptiles. Trout, salmon, and other creatures died in ash-choked lakes and streams.

NATURAL RECOVERY

In 1982, about 11,000 acres (4,452 ha) around the mountain became a new park, the Mount St. Helens National Volcanic Monument. The Forest Service planted seeds and spread fertilizer on the bare slopes. They hoped that grass and shrubs would hold the soil together to prevent it from **eroding**. They mainly left nature to recover by itself, however. Scientists were surprised at the speed of the recovery. As early as autumn 1980, plants such as fireweed

23

MEASURING ERUPTIONS

One way of determining the size of a volcano's eruption is to measure the total amount of ash and rock that is blown into the air. Scientists call this material the volcano's ejecta. In 1980, Mount St. Helens spouted 0.24 cubic miles (1 cubic kilometer) of ejecta, which is a small amount compared to giant eruptions of the past. The 1815 eruption of Mount Tambora in Indonesia released an incredible 19.2 cubic miles (80 cu km) of ejecta, and its ash cloud spread around the world. It partly blocked the sun's rays for several years, lowering temperatures all around the globe.

▼ Smoke, ash, and rock billow from Mount St. Helens. The huge cloud rose into the air for nine hours and spread eastward at a speed of 60 miles (96 km) per hour.

▲ Fireweed grows on Mount St. Helens in August 1984. Seeds for the new plants were blown into the area by the wind, or carried there by animals.

and lupine had begun to reappear on the gray slopes. Other plants were soon growing there, too.

The damage caused by the eruption was less serious than experts first feared. For example, the damage to wild plants and farm crops was lessened by the timing of the eruption, which happened in spring. High on the mountain, thick snow still protected some seeds and saplings. Even though many animals died, some of the animals that were hibernating were protected by their burrows and shelters. Lower down, most crops and fruit trees were at a point in their growing cycles when they could better survive a thick coating of ash.

In the months after the eruption, logging companies began planting new trees to replace the many thousands of trees knocked down on the mountain. The first, quick-growing trees were cut for logging in the late 1990s.

U.S. Army **engineers** worked to prevent erosion and flooding. They dug a tunnel for floodwater from Spirit Lake to prevent rising waters from setting off mudflows. A new road now runs to Coldwater Ridge, where David Johnston died. It leads to a new tourist center named for the young scientist.

ADVANCES IN VOLCANOLOGY

Mount St. Helens was a good lesson in how to deal with a volcanic eruption. Officials sealed off the area when the eruption was close, which saved many lives. Since then, geologists have learned to predict eruptions even better.

► These bear tracks in the ash were a sign that even large animals were returning to the mountain. They were photographed only five months after the eruption.

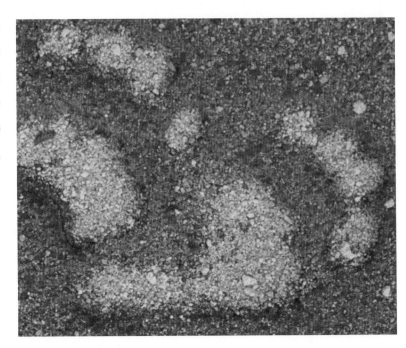

LIFE RETURNS TO THE MOUNTAIN

All parts of Mount St. Helens have now begun to recover from the 1980 eruption. Young willow and alder trees have taken root in the upper valley of the Toutle River, which was destroyed by an avalanche of mud and debris. Flowering plants have bloomed, and animals are also returning. Birds, insects, and mice are nesting in fallen trees in the blasted zone, while frogs, toads, and fish swim again in lakes and streams. Even large beasts such as bears, elk, and deer have returned and are increasing in numbers.

▼ A herd of elk roams on Mount St. Helens in February 1986. A law against hunting encouraged wildlife to come back to the mountainside.

In 1985, a new emergency service, the Volcano Disaster Assistance Program (VDAP) was founded after a disaster in the Andes Mountains in South America. When a volcano named Nevado del Ruiz erupted, a mudflow swamped the town of Armero. Twenty-three thousand people died. Volcanologists believed that many deaths could have been avoided if

NEW LANDSCAPES

The land around Mount St. Helens was greatly changed by the eruption. Two new lakes, Coldwater Lake and Castle Lake, formed when debris from the eruption dammed mountain streams. Spirit Lake is much bigger than before. It is fed by a new waterfall, Loowit Falls, which channels water from the mountain's crater. Within the crater itself, a new dome has started to rise, fed by rising magma. By 2005, the dome stood over 330 feet (100 m) high and was continuing to grow. The big question: How often will its growth be halted by future eruptions?

▼ **Castle Lake was created when debris from the Mount St. Helens eruption blocked a river. Engineers have made the natural dam across the lake stronger so that it is safe.**

officials had moved people out of the area sooner. Now, VDAP scientists regularly offer advice to countries where eruptions threaten.

In 1991, the VDAP team flew to the island of Luzon in the Philippines, where a volcano named Pinatubo was showing danger signs. The area was **evacuated**, which saved many

▲ **Before: The graceful shape of Mount St. Helens before the 1980 eruption.**

▼ **After: The new lava dome rises in the hole left in the mountain after the eruption of 1980.**

lives when Pinatubo blew on June 15 with a force even greater than the Mount St. Helens eruption.

THE MOUNTAIN AWAKENS

After a long quiet period, in September 2004, Mount St. Helens became more active than at any time since the 1980 eruption. Geologists said that it might be on the verge of erupting again. The next month, small eruptions threw ash and steam into the air, but no lava. Visitors were evacuated from a 5-mile (8-km) zone around the volcano.

Scientists waited to see if the volcano would settle down, or if the activity was the start of a major eruption. Even if the mountain did blow, they said, the blast would not be nearly as powerful as the great 1980 blast.

GLOSSARY

active Related to a volcano that might erupt; volcanoes that are not likely to erupt are called inactive, or dormant, volcanoes.

crater A deep, basin-shaped hole at the peak of a volcano.

debris Pieces left when something has been broken up or destroyed.

ecologists Scientists who study living things and how they relate to where they live.

engineers People who are trained to work with engines or to make and build things.

eroding Wearing away, such as the wearing away of rock by the wind or by moving water.

erupt To force out or release, often suddenly and violently. When a volcano erupts, it shoots out gas, lava, and ash.

evacuate To move people out of a dangerous area.

geological Related to geology; geology is the study of soil, rocks, and minerals and what they tell us about the history of Earth.

molten Related to being melted. The word is often used to describe super-hot rock that flows like a liquid.

mudflows Water or melted snow that combines with soil to become moving flows of mud.

National Guard A branch of the U.S. military that is only active when called upon by a state or by the federal government.

subduction zone A place where one of Earth's tectonic plates slips beneath another. These zones often feature many volcanoes.

tectonic Related to the crust of a planet, such as Earth.

tiltmeter A scientific tool that is used to measure the angle of Earth's surface.

FURTHER RESEARCH

BOOKS

Ball, Jacqueline A. *Volcanoes.* (Discovery Channel School Science) Gareth Stevens Publishing, 2004.

Bredeson, Carmen. *Mount St. Helens Volcano: Violent Eruption.* (American Disasters) Enslow Publishers, 2001.

Nicholson, Cynthia Pratt. *Volcano!* (Disaster). Kids Can Press, 2001.

Rose, Susanna Van. *Volcano.* (Eyewitness Books) Dorling Kindersley, 2004.

Spilsbury, Louise. *Violent Volcanoes.* (Awesome Forces of Nature) Heinemann Library, 2004.

Sutherland, Lin. *Earthquakes & Volcanoes.* (Reader's Digest) Reader's Digest, 2003.

WEB SITES

Cascades Volcano Observatory, Vancouver
vulcan.wr.usgs.gov/volcanoes/MSH/NatMonument/framework.html

Exploring the Environment: Volcanoes, Center for Educational Technologies
www.cotf.edu/ete/modules/volcanoes/vnarrative1.html

Forces of Nature: Volcanoes, National Geographic
www.nationalgeographic.com/forcesofnature/interactive/index.html?section=h

Mount St. Helens National Volcanic Monument.
www.fs.fed.us/gpnf/mshnvm

Savage Planet: Volcanic Killers
www.pbs.org.wnet/savageplanet/01volcano/02/indexmid.html/

INDEX